D1467626

to: _____

from: _____

If you … know how to give good gifts to your children,
how much more will your Father in heaven
give good gifts to those who ask him!

MATTHEW 7:11

Prayers from a Dad's Heart

Copyright © 2003 by Robert Wolgemuth
ISBN 0-310-98794-6

Requests for information should be addressed to:
Inspirio, The gift group of Zondervan
Grand Rapids, Michigan 49530
http://www.inspiriogifts.com

Editor: Janice Jacobson
Design Manager: Amy J. Wenger
Design: The Office of Bill Chiaravalle, DeAnna Pierce I www.officeofbc.com

Printed in China
03 04 05/HK/ 4 3 2 1

Prayers

FROM A

DAD'S HEART

BY ROBERT WOLGEMUTH

inspirio™

Dr. Samuel Frey Wolgemuth

1914-2002

He loved God.
He loved his family.
He prayed on his knees.
He prayed from his heart.

Introduction

Welcome to this book of stories and prayers.

You and I may have very little in common except for one thing—
we are men with a child of our own. And for the time being, that's
good enough.

It's my sincere hope that you'll find this little book to be an
encouragement as you pray for your child or children…and
yourself, a man yanked from the ranks of the unprepared and
given the assignment of being a dad.

But that's okay. Even though we are both still in the process of
learning about this awesome task, my prayer is that you will be

inspired to establish the habit of praying for your children—by name, every day. And I hope that you will do this on your knees. This is something I learned from my own dad who—just like you and me—must have been overwhelmed with both the blessing and the responsibility of being a godly father.

Praying for your children should not be drudgery; it should be an adventure. It is, after all, the spine-tingling delight of ushering your children into the throne room of the living God.

May the Holy Spirit guide you as you launch—through your own example—a legacy of prayer and a heritage of faith.

Table of Contents

TRIBUTE *to a*
PRAYING DAD

The Picture

With a dad like mine, I didn't stand a chance.

A decade ago I was sitting in the office of one of our town's most highly respected litigators. We were talking about the possibility of my filing a lawsuit against someone who had wronged me. "I'm confident enough about your chances that I'll take your case on a contingency," the lawyer said.

My heart raced. This could mean a lot of money and I knew it. But what would the next two years be like? I'd be taking on men I know—in some cases, friends. I told the attorney that I'd think about. Even pray about it.

Late that afternoon as I turned my car into my driveway I knew that I couldn't go through with the lawsuit. I couldn't take friends to court? No settlement would be worth this.

Take friends to court? With a dad like mine, I didn't stand a chance.

About a decade before that, I was faced with the perfect opportunity to be unfaithful to my wife and family. I had made all the rationalizations a man could make, and the situation was presenting itself in an ideal setting. I had one last chance to think about it before making the mistake of a lifetime. I walked away from temptation.

With a dad like mine, I didn't stand a chance.

A couple of decades before that I was a college student. Like lots of men my age, I was pushing the edges on what I knew was right. I was confident that no one—especially my father—would find out about his rebellious boy. I was wrong.

The day after Thanksgiving, 1966, my dad asked me if we could "have a talk." We walked into his bedroom. He sat down on a chair in the corner of the room, and began to tell me that he had "heard a few things about my activities at school." Then instead of making demands or issuing threats, my dad confessed that he had spent too much time on the road when I was in high school. The president of an international youth ministry at the time, he offered to quit his job. I would move back home and enroll in a local junior college.

"We'll spend a year together and I can make up for some of our lost time," he said to me, tears welling up in his eyes.

A few minutes later, I trudged down the hall to my bedroom, completely shaken with what I had just experienced. How could I break my father's heart?

With a dad like mine, I didn't stand a chance.

Today I'm a grown man—a husband, father and grandfather. My dad is in heaven. I can no longer hear his voice on the telephone. "Much better, now that I'm talking to you," he'd say when I'd ask him how he was.

Almost every day, I'm faced with temptations to lie, cheat, steal, slander, gossip, and lust. But with a dad like mine, I don't stand a chance.

When I was a little boy, I was often wakened in the darkness of the early morning hours with the sound of my dad praying. His deep voice sent a quiet but audible vibration through our house. My brothers and sisters and I knew that we were being named, one at a time: Ruth, Sam, Ken, Robert, Debbie, Dan. Faithfully, from his knees, he would bring us before his heavenly Father and plead our case. We knew that he prayed for our protection from harm and our obedience to God's voice.

This is why, with a dad like mine, I didn't stand a chance.

This is a book of stories and prayers for you, a man with children of your own. It's my hope that you'll find it a helpful guide as you pray for your kids.

My prayer for you is that this book will get you into the habit of praying for your children—by name, every day. My hope is that you'll also do this on your knees. What you'll be providing for your children is exactly what my dad did for me.

A few months before he died, I sat with my dad in his home. He was suffering from a rare neurological disease that rendered him quiet and withdrawn. He had a hard time talking or listening. His eyes were failing so he couldn't read or watch the Cubs or Bulls on television.

"Dad," I said to him. "How does all of this make you feel?"

He looked straight into my eyes. "Useless," he said.

"Dad," I finally said after a few minutes. "Do you remember how you used to pray for us?"

"I still do," he returned with a faint smile.

"Do you know what a difference that makes in our lives? Do you know how thankful we are?"

He nodded.

"Even if you were able-bodied and strong," I continued, "there still is nothing more important—more useful—than you could do than to continue to pray."

"You're right … thank you, son," my dad added.

"No, thank you," I said as I walked over to his chair. Kneeling down in front of my dad I put my arms around him.

"Thank you," I repeated, kissing him on the cheek. I held him for just a few more moments and kissed him again.

With a dad like mine, I didn't stand a chance.

Great is the LORD and most worthy of praise;
His greatness no one can fathom.
One generation will commend your works to another;
they will tell of your might acts.

PSALM 145:3, 4

The Prayers

A Prayer *for* You

Father in Heaven,

Thank you for the blessing of a praying father. His commitment to consistent and specific prayer for me throughout my life has helped me to reach beyond myself and provided me with the wisdom to take hold of your promises. My father's prayers urged me to follow your perfect will for my life.

Help me Lord, to be as faithful to pray for my child as my father prayed for me. Help me to establish a special time when I can come before you for each of my children. And father, I pray that you will strengthen me as I undertake this important responsibility. Help me always to model right living in their lives.

I pray in Jesus' name,

Amen

A Prayer *for* Your Child

Father in Heaven,

Thank you for blessing the life of my child. Thank you for the plan you have in place for her. I pray that she will listen to your voice and follow your lead. Keep her steps on the path to righteousness and her heart devoted to pleasing you. I pray that you will surround her with wise and godly counselors and instruct her through your Word.

I pray in Jesus' name,

Amen.

Children have more need of model than of critics.

Joseph Joubert

A CONUNDRUM FOR SURE

The Promise

My son, do not make light of the Lord's discipline,
and do not lose heart when he rebukes you,
because the Lord disciplines those he loves,
and he punishes everyone he accepts as a son.
Endure hardship as discipline; God is treating you as sons.
For what son is not disciplined by his father?

HEBREWS 12:5–7

The Picture

"I really want to love my kids … and I want them to love me."

What dad hasn't had this thought as he watches his kids grow up? This is the goal.

One fall afternoon several years ago, my wife, Bobbie and I were traveling south in Pennsylvania between Danville and Harrisburg. We had just visited with my wife's parents and we were on our way to the airport in Harrisburg.

It was one of those autumn days when the sky is cloudless, giving the sun a chance to turn up the volume on all the colors. To our left was the mighty Susquehanna River snaking along in tandem with the highway. To our right were tree-covered hillsides, small towns and farms.

In the distance, we—mostly Bobbie—spotted a two-story frame house with large blankets hanging from clotheslines. As we got closer, we—mostly Bobbie—realized that these were not blankets but quilts—handmade quilts.

"Robert," Bobbie pleaded. "Quilts. Could we stop this time? Please?"

We were making record time. According to my calculations since leaving Danville, we had averaged just under 60 miles per hour—pretty stout for a mostly two-lane road. The way I figured it, we were close to breaking our all-time record.

I lifted my foot from the accelerator and touched the brake.[1]

We pulled onto the shoulder and turned slowly up the driveway. The crunch of the gravel under my tires took me back to visits to my own grandparents' homes in Lancaster County, not too far from where we were. Two plainly dressed women met us at the back door. They were friendly, but guarded. The younger women looked about 18. The other woman must have been her mother.

When we stepped into the kitchen, the smell of a burning coal oil stove filled the air. I looked over to the kitchen sink. The plumbing fixtures from the double sink had been removed and a white plastic bucket was sitting in one of them. A large unlit gas lantern sat on the kitchen table.

The women led us to a large room filled with folding tables. On each table were quilts—beautiful handmade masterpieces of every imaginable size—piled high: placemats, teapot covers, baby quilts, medium-sized quilts. Huge colorful quilts covered the walls that surrounded us. Bobbie gasped in awe. I was glad that we had stopped. It was okay that the record time to Harrisburg would have to wait for another trip.

One by one, the women took us to the tables, explaining the patterns. Bobbie stopped often to examine the intricate needlework. "Who made these?" she asked. The 18-year-old smiled and blushed. She glanced to the floor. "We made them," the mother answered. "Some of our friends have helped … but mostly we made them."

We stood there for just a moment, drinking it all in. Then after a few more tables of quilts, I glanced at my watch. Bobbie caught the cue and picked out a few crib-sized quilts that "would be perfect gifts for baby showers."

As we were walking to the car, I heard the clopping of horseshoes and the squeaks of a cart. A boy of about 16 was driving a large flat cart. The bed was piled high with hay. I smiled at him. He smiled, nodded and touched the brim of his hat.

As we headed for Harrisburg, Bobbie asked a question: "The teenagers we just met live a highly disciplined lifestyle. They work hard and are given none of the frills available to other American teens—perks like cars, trendy clothes, the latest electronics, or pocket money. Do you think their parents love them more or less than other American parents love their children?"

It's an interesting conundrum for sure. What is the proper balance? God treats his own children with a blend of hard-nosed discipline and compelling love. That must be the formula he expects us to use as well.

The LORD *disciplines those he loves,*
as a father the son he delights in.

PROVERBS 3:12

The Prayers

A PRAYER *for* YOU

Father in Heaven,

Thank you for providing hard work for me to set my hand to. Thank you for disciplining me as the son you love by letting me endure certain hardships. I want to welcome tough times because they teach me to lean on you and love you even more. You are my example of a father with perfect balance between withholding and giving, between discipline and grace. Help me to demonstrate what I have received from you by compelling my child by your standard. Help me delight in my son by watching carefully all his activities and accumulations. Help me make the difficult decision to give him what he really needs and not just what he wants. For this task I need your discernment, your confidence and knowledge from your Word.

I pray in Jesus' name.

Amen.

A Prayer *for* Your Child

Father in Heaven,

Thank you for providing hard work and simple tasks to set my child's hands to. Help him to balance fun and work in his life. When solicitors try to capture his mind and emotions with things that do not promote good character, compel him by your Spirit and with my love and admonitions to do the right thing. Help him feel the delight I have in him and the love we have together in this partnership.

I pray in Jesus' name.

Amen.

When God chastises his children,
he does not punish as a judge does;
but he chastens as a father.

C.H. Spurgeon

AND in YOUR PURITY

The Promise

Don't let anyone look down on you because you are young,
But set an example for the believers
In speech, in life, in love, in faith and in purity.

1 TIMOTHY 4:12

The Picture

I am the father of two daughters. As they grew into young women, I began to get a little nervous. Of course, I had no idea what it was like to be a teenage girl, but I *did* know what it was like to be a teenage *boy*, if you know what I mean.

There were two things stacked in my favor during those years:

1) I had spent almost seven years in youth ministry, working with high school kids and their families. This experience taught me how to talk to young people with absolute honesty. It also proved to me that this was what they preferred; and

2) I have a wife who is a truth-teller. She is also a woman who believes in the priceless worth of purity.

I remember when the girls graduated from their cribs and began to sleep in big-girl beds. Each night as they knelt beside those beds with Bobbie and me for nighttime prayers, they heard us pray for "the little boys somewhere in the world who would grow up to be their husbands."

It makes me smile remembering how detailed our prayers were, "Lord, please help those little boys—wherever they are—to be safe when they rides their bikes. Help them to obey their mothers and dads. Help them to learn to love you. Amen."

Sometimes our girls would talk about these little boys. Their imaginations were vivid. "I hope he didn't fall off his bike today," Julie said as we pulled her covers up to her chin.

Years later our daughters had a conversation with a radiant new wife, less than one year into her marriage. She told them that, years before, she had made a list of qualities she was looking for in a husband.

They were inspired by her story and sat down to do the same thing. Their lists were exhaustive and detailed. And once they saw how special their grooms were going to be, they determined that it was only right to prepare themselves for such a wonderful man.

As each of my daughters reached the age of 16, I did my best to take my proper place in their dating adventure. With their permission, I interviewed the young men who came to take them out. This was not a screening process. Every boy passed.[1]

My duty was *not* to help Missy or Julie to decide whether this suitor was acceptable. My job was simply to sit down with the young men and find out about them—their goals, their interests, their families.

I told each young man that he was welcome in our home. And it was my goal to help him understand that the young woman in question, my daughter, was part of a family who loved her very much. I also mentioned that Mrs. Wolgemuth and I talked about everything with our daughters— that they willingly shared every detail of their activities with us when they came home from being out with friends or on a date.

This last comment always caught the young men's attention.

It didn't take too long for me to realize that there were some boys out there who hadn't made lists of their own.

One of our daughters told us about a conversation she had with a boy who had fallen for her after several dates. Through tears he had said to her, "If I had known that there would be a girl like you, I would have waited and kept my purity. Now I know that it's too late."

I remember exactly how I felt when I heard this. I was glad that our girls had given us permission to be involved in this part of their lives.

Years later, our Julie was working with the high school kids at our church. One evening, a sobbing teenage girl told her that she had agreed to have sex with her boyfriend for his sixteenth birthday. "Why did you do that?" Julie asked.

"Because nobody told me not to," the girl answered.

Your job as the father of a girl or a boy is to protect and advise—to remind your children of what the Apostle Paul wrote to his protégé. "Be an example," he told young Timothy, "in the way you talk, the way you live, the way you love, the way you believe . . . and in your purity." Pray for your children's mates. Challenge them to be pure. And give them a chance to see what this looks like in your own life.

Dear friends, let us purify ourselves
from everything that contaminates body and spirit,
Perfecting holiness out of reverence for God.

2 CORINTHIANS 7:1

The Prayers

A PRAYER *for* YOU

Father in Heaven,

You are the creator of love and marriage and have provided the most fulfilling expression of true love. Thank you for giving us perfect guidelines. Help me to be pure in my own thought, life and activities. Then, I ask for your wisdom as I prepare my child for her future. With absolute honesty help me to help my child envision the purity possible for her life. Help me to be a protector by making sure that every person she dates sees her as part of a loving family and in a relationship with a holy God. I accept the challenge of being the example and advisor my child needs. For this task, I need your ideas, your discernment and your Spirit's power.

In the strong name of the only one who can keep us from falling, Jesus Christ.

Amen.

A Prayer *for* Your Child

Father in Heaven,

You designed my child to be loved and fulfilled. As we pray together about her future mate, give her a picture of the grand idea of a loving companion who holds purity in highest regard. Help my child to list the qualities of the spouse she is willing to wait for. I ask for friends who will support my child in her decision to be pure. Then, by the power of your Spirit, I pray that you will allow my child to be an example in life, love, faith, and purity. This prayer is for my child's future and for your glory.

In the strong name of the only one who can keep her from falling, Jesus Christ.

Amen.

Vigilance and prayer are the safeguards of chastity.

St. Jean Baptist de la Salle

ARE YOU FUN
to LIVE WITH?

The Promise

A cheerful look brings joy to the heart,
And good news gives health to the bones.

PROVERBS 15:30

The Picture

Two gas company servicemen, a senior training supervisor and a young trainee, were out checking meters in a suburban neighborhood. They parked their truck at the end of the alley and worked their way to the other end. At the last house an elderly woman watched from her kitchen window as they checked her gas meter.

Finishing the meter check, the senior supervisor challenged his younger coworker to a foot race down the alley back to the truck.

As they came running up to the truck, they realized the lady from that last house was huffing and puffing right behind them. They stopped and asked her what was wrong.

Gasping for breath, she replied, "When I see two gas men running from my house as hard as you two were, I figured I'd better get out while I can!"

Don't you just love to laugh? I do, too.

Bobbie and I had been married for less than two years when one of our couple-friends invited us to a workshop. The leader's name was Dr. Lionel Whiston, and he was going to talk about his new book, *Are You Fun to Live With?* We hadn't heard of Dr. Whiston or his book, but we agreed to go. An evening with these friends wouldn't be a waste of time, regardless.

We were in for a wonderful surprise. I remember being captivated by Dr. Whiston. His pure white hair and stature spoke of elegance and grace. His infectious smile warmed the room. On our way home, I told Bobbie that I had an answer to the question Dr. Whiston's book posed.

At least for me, the answer was "no." I wasn't fun to live with, and I knew it. Bobbie didn't disagree. The confession felt good.

We were pregnant with our first baby and that night I resolved that I was going to do my best to be a dad who was fun to live with—for the rest of my life.

The problem, it seems, is that I'm fifth generation German-American. My ancestors on my father's side—especially the men—were dead serious about life. Their work, their religion, their personal discipline, their family life, and their demeanor were stoic and temperate. They were even serious about their humor.

When something funny was said or done, their response was a raised eyebrow and thin smile. "Now that's quite amusing, Hiram," one of them might say. And then they'd get back to work. Belly laughs were as scarce as hen's teeth.[1]

This German sense of humor was spot-welded to my DNA. If someone had surveyed the people who knew me well, they might say something like, "He's a nice guy, lovely wife and good teeth . . . but frankly, he's a little boring."

Something had to change.

So I began to earnestly collect funny things: riddle books, comic strips (*The Far Side* was my favorite), and books of humor. I subscribed to The *Reader's Digest* and found it full of treasures. I'd take quips and anecdotes and try them out in my Sunday school lessons and at home. They worked like a charm . . . ·

> *A cheerful heart is good medicine,*
> *But a crushed spirit dries up the bones.*

PROVERBS 17:22

Even the Bible confirms what I'm saying.

As our children grew, humor became like glue binding us together. Laughter around the kitchen table or playing "monster on the landing" eased the drudgery of the daily grind. Giggles and squeals filled our house. These times lifted our spirits.

There may be no more sober story in all of Scripture than the story of Job. In a matter of a few days, he went from the most prosperous and exemplary man in the region to the most tragic and pitiable.

At the height of his lamenting, he discovered something astonishing—something that seems completely out of character. This is what Job said:

When I smiled at them, they scarcely believed it;
the light of my face was precious to them.

JOB 29:24

No one had ever suffered more than he, but Job found release in a smile. This made his face shine and his friends were drawn to him. If ever there were a legitimate case for sobriety and gloom, it was his. But Job smiled, and it worked.

Are you fun to live with? If you're not sure of the answer, go ask your wife and kids. Tell them that there will be no reprisal or punishment for a truthful answer. Then tell them about the time you went to a new chicken restaurant. You walked up to the counter and asked how they prepare their chickens.

The kid behind the cash register looked up and smiled. "We just tell them they're going to die."

If your family admits that you're not all that fun to live with, don't you think it's time to do something about it?[2]

The Prayers

A PRAYER *for* YOU

Father in Heaven,

You have created so many things for our enjoyment. It is fun to look at some of your humor in the wildlife and fish you have made. You made smiles and laughter. I want to be part of the fun, especially with my family. I pray for a lighter heart so I can be a dad who is fun to live with for the rest of my life. I want humor to be one of the things that lifts our spirits and binds us together at home. Please let the light of my face be an encouragement to my family.

In the strength of Your Joy,

Amen.

A Prayer *for* Your Child

Father in Heaven,

Thank you for the infectious laugh and the delightful spirit you have given my child. The radiant smiles that I love to see are a clear picture of your joy. Help my child cultivate happiness by choosing to look on the bright side of your design. Help him decide to be fun to live with, especially at home. Like good medicine, help my child find good jokes and funny stories to spread cheer wherever he goes. Bless him with the joy of your presence as his strength.

In the strength of your joy,

Amen

It is the soul that is not yet sure of its God that is afraid to laugh in His presence.

George MacDonald

EXPECT *and* INSPECT

The Promise

The Israelites had done all the work
just as the LORD had commanded Moses.
Moses inspected the work and saw that they had done it
just as the LORD had commanded.
So Moses blessed them.

EXODUS 39:42

The Picture

The great Zig Ziglar tells the story of growing up in Yazoo City, Mississippi. His daddy died when Zig was five, and his mother was left alone to raise eight children. Zig describes his mother as a tough, no-nonsense woman, who stood no more than five feet, two inches tall.

One hot summer afternoon, Mrs. Ziglar told Zig to hoe a row of beans. It was his job to dig around each plant with a garden hoe, overturning the soil and dislodging any weeds that had grown there. As he looked down the row, it stretched out for 3 miles—at least that's how it seemed to an eight-year-old boy!

Zig dug in. Hoeing and digging until the job was finished. He went to his mother to announce that he was done.

Mrs. Ziglar put on her bonnet and walked to the row of beans. She looked up and down the row, her head slowly shaking from side to side. "This work may be good enough for some boys," she said without looking up, "but you're not *some* boys—you're *my* boy." She handed Zig the hoe, turned and walked back into the house. Zig's mother *expected* her boy to do a good job; then she *inspected* the work, just to be sure.

My dad was like Zig's mother. My childhood assignment wasn't hoeing three miles of beans, but it was mowing seven acres of grass—at least that's what it looked like to me.

I can remember grumbling to myself as I pushed the mower back and forth.

When I finished, my dad would walk the yard, inspecting my work. Incredibly, between the time I pushed the lawnmower into the garage and the time my dad slowly walked across the grass, some "skippers" always appeared. It seemed perfect when I finished, but when dad looked it over, thin slices of lawn seemed to be calling out, "Yoo-hoo, over here!"

Samuel Wolgemuth didn't use the same words Zig Ziglar's mother used, but he made a *tsk-tsk* noise with his tongue on the roof of his mouth, signaling his disappointment. I knew that meant I had more work to do so I would trudge to the garage, fire up the mower, and go over it again. My dad *expected* me to do a good job, then he *inspected* my work.

As youngsters, you could not have convinced Zig and me that our parents were doing anything but harassing us. *Why don't you let us play ball like our friends*, we mumbled to ourselves as we fixed our work. Today, I know differently. Mrs. Ziglar and Dr. Wolgemuth were saying to little Zig and little Robert, "I love you."

The children of Israel were somewhere between Egypt and Canaan—slavery and the Promised Land. During the 40 years of waiting to return to their homeland, the Lord gave Moses instructions to build the Ark of the Covenant—intended to hold the ten commandments—and the Tabernacle—a collapsible, portable temple. Moses gave the people their assignments.[1]

When they were finished with their work, Moses went for a walk. Can't you see these people nervously watching the great patriarch examining their handiwork? Moses knew what Mrs. Ziglar and my dad knew. If you *expect* your children to do the work, don't forget to *inspect* the final product.

A huge sigh of relief must have been audible at the site when Moses looked over the work and found it to be just as the Lord had commanded.[2]

Because he was pleased with the people's efforts, Moses did something remarkable. He didn't just tell them that they had done well, nor did he congratulate them with a celebration. (Actually, he *may* have done these things, but it's not recorded here.) Moses called for silence and faced the people. He lifted his hands heavenward and blessed them, his voice booming across the plain and careening off the foothills of Mount Sinai.

The LORD your God will bless you
in the land he is giving you.

DEUTERONOMY 28:8

Can't you feel what the people must have felt? They had successfully finished a big assignment and their leader was pleased—really pleased. His words told them what Zig and I heard when our parents came back to look at our work the second time. "Good job, son. Good work, son. I'm proud of you, son" . . . oh yes, and "I love you, son."

When you give your children their assignments, expect them to do their best. Then carefully inspect their work. This will be a great gift. When they've done well and hear it from you, they will grow in self-respect. That's important because some day soon they will inspect their own work. And they'll have learned how to do it from you.

> *Whatever you do, work at it with all your heart,*
>
> *as working for the Lord, not for men.*

COLOSSIANS 3:23

The Prayers

A Prayer *for* You

Father in Heaven,

Thank you for giving me assignments and keeping track of my work. Help me to do everything I do with the excellence that honors you. I want to know that you are pleased with me. Give me wisdom as I give responsibility to my child. Help me to expect the best and inspect her work. Let her hear me say, "Good job" and "I love you" often. Thank you for the privilege you have given me to cultivate good habits in my child that will help her be a successful adult. I need your help to accomplish this very large task. Please inspect my work.

For your glory.

Amen.

A Prayer *for* Your Child

Father in Heaven,

Thank you for the tasks that teach my child about hard work and doing a good job. Build good habits and self- respect in my child as I encourage her by expecting, inspecting and praising her work. Help my child see that she is special and nothing less than her best will be acceptable. Encourage her through me when we are struggling against sloppy ways and shoddy work. Together, we bring our best to you. Thank you for the blessings you promise when we do our work for you.

Your will be done, through us, as it is in Heaven.

Amen

Always do more than is required of you.

John Wooden

FAMILY
SECRETS

The Promise

He who dwells in the secret place of the Most High
shall abide under the shadow of the Almighty.
I will say of the Lord, "He is my refuge and my fortress;
my God, in Him I will trust."

PSALM 91:1–2

The Picture

Last year, Bobbie and I started making a list. Our first plan was to give each of our adult daughters a pillowcase for Christmas with the things on this list written with indelible ink. Then, we realized that the list was too long for a pillowcase. Plus, we wanted the list to be more permanent than that.

After a year, we still haven't decided how we're going to present the list to Missy and Julie, but I'm sure we'll think of something. It may be a tablecloth or a quilt. What do you think?

But wait a minute. I haven't told you what's on the list. It's our family secrets.

By "secrets" I don't mean intimate things or skeletons in the closet that aren't anyone's business. No, this is a collection of sentences, sayings, moments, movie lines, and codes that mean something to our family. We've been collecting these for thirty years and we have over a hundred of them.

When our two sons-in-law joined the family, we told them all about our family secrets and that we were going to give them a test on their meanings. But we haven't done that yet.

Here are a few of them...

"Bickla or Grunder"—When Bobbie was pregnant with our second child, these were the names our three-year old chose for her new brother or sister. We had no idea where she got them nor did we know which was the name for a girl and which was for a boy. As our daughters have had children of their own, "Bickla" and "Grunder" are always on their list of possibilities.

"Make quick decisions"—The girls were teenagers, and we were wandering through the "Junior" department at Dillards. My patience was running out. I gathered my family together, like a quarterback calling a play, and with a karate chop motion with one hand on the palm of the other, I "ordered" my wife and daughters to "make quick decisions." They stepped back in amazement that anyone would try to spoil their adventure, and then broke out in side-splitting laughter. For the past twenty years, whenever my family sees me growing impatient . . . about anything, they'll say, "We know, Dad. Make quick decisions."

"Go get Doc Baker!"—"Little House on the Prairie" was one of our favorite television programs. In case you don't remember the show, Charles and Caroline Ingalls and their family lived in Walnut Grove, Minnesota at the end of the 19th century. And in almost every episode someone got sick or hurt. The town physician was Dr. Hiram Baker and, of course, he made house calls. "Go get Doc Baker!" someone would holler. For the past twenty years, whenever something happens in our family that may have required urgent attention—real or imagined—one of us will say, "Go get Doc Baker!" Sometimes the laughter that follows magically fixes the problem.

"143-31"—We commandeered this family secret from my brother, Dan, and his family's list of secrets. It's one of my favorites. I carry a digital pager. When someone in my family wants to send me a secret message, they dial my pager number and punch in "1—4—3" and their age. These numbers represent "I love you" and the age identifies the message sender. In this case "3-1" would be our older daughter, Missy.

You may want to start a list of your own family secrets. They'll give you years of memories and fun. Our secrets have provided us with lots of laughter. And—this may sound silly—these little family secrets have bound us together with a special identity.

Did you know that God's family is bound together by a secret? When new members join His family, they're introduced to this great mystery. The wonder of his love and mercy fastens them to each other with unbreakable cords.

Oh, how great is God's goodness,
which He has laid up for those who fear Him,
which He has prepared for those who trust in Him....
God shall hide them in the secret place of His presence ...
He shall keep them secretly in a pavilion.

PSALM 31:19,20 NKJV

In the same way that "Go get Doc Baker" and "143-31" mean something special to our family, the miracle of God's grace gives members of his family a mysterious strength—a secret hope. God's family secrets give his children a reason for living.

By the way, the difference between "family secrets" and real secrets is that it's okay to tell non-family members about these. Family secrets are meant to be shared.[1]

> *The friendship of the Lord is for those who fear him.*
> *And he makes his covenant known to them.*

PSALM 25:14 NRSV

The Prayers

A PRAYER *for* YOU

Father in Heaven,

Thank you for opening up the secret place of your presence as my place of rest and safety. I am unworthy of friendship with you, yet you invite me to be your friend. You share the secrets of your kingdom with me. How remarkable. I trust in you. I revere your name. Tell me what you want me to know today about your covenant love. I will share your secrets with my family.

In your trustworthy name I pray,

Amen.

A Prayer *for* Your Child

Father in Heaven,

Thank you for your love and friendship with my child. Thank you for being a shelter for my child so she can live under the shadow of the Almighty. You share secrets with your family members. As my child learns to trust in you, please reveal to her the promises and special mysteries of your covenant love. Bond my child to you with the strength of secrets from the inside circle. And fasten her to our family with unbreakable cords of love, too.

In secret hope I pray,

Amen.

FOR JUST ONE WEEKEND

The Promise

Then the word of the Lord came to Jeremiah:

"I am the Lord, the God of all mankind.

Is anything too hard for me?"

The Picture

It happened almost every Sunday afternoon before our daughters grew up and moved away from home.

We'd curl up on the couch together and watch the magic professional golfers could work with golf clubs. The beauty of the world's most fantastic country clubs and the subdued tone of the announcers' voices were a perfect combination for a lazy Sunday afternoon. This ritual became known as "Golf on TV."

As a golfer, I carry an 18 handicap. If I break 90[1], I pump my fists and dance around on the eighteenth green like I've just won the Masters. My friends hurry off to the locker room, denying any association with the guy doing the two-step.

But, even though I'm not very good at the game, I truly love it. In fact, on those quiet Sunday afternoons, I still watch "Golf on TV" alone. Sometimes I daydream. It goes something like this . . .

A few months before the U.S. Open I send a letter to the PGA. I explain that, although I'm an 18 handicapper, I would sincerely appreciate an opportunity to try out. For some reason, the official who opens the letter has an unusual wave of complicity sweep over him, and he gives me the green light.

When the tryouts begin in my local area, I grab my clubs and go for it. From the time I step onto the first tee-box in the first qualifying tournament, I'm amazing. The best drive I've ever hit, the best fairway wood I've ever taken, the best short iron I've ever struck, and my most accurate putt, happen all day—hole after hole.

The weekend of the Open approaches. I get what I've been dreaming of—an official invitation to compete as an amateur.

Now it's Thursday morning. I've been to the practice range and putting green and now I'm walking toward the grandstands that surround the first tee. Thousands of people are watching, not counting worldwide television coverage. And yet, I'm completely calm.

As I walk past the spectators standing behind the ropes, I hear people say, "Who's that guy?" I smile, nod, and touch the bill of my cap like I've seen the big boys do so many times.

"From his favorite public course in Orlando, Florida … Robert Wolgemuth," the starter announces over the loudspeaker, doing his best to sound excited to say my name. "Polite" describes the applause, at best. I see people in the grandstands leaning into each other to talk. I can't hear what they're saying, but that doesn't matter. I already know.

I nod and touch the bill of my cap again. I tee the ball up, take a few practice swings, and take my stance. I remain totally calm. The only emotion I can feel is anticipation.

I draw my club back and begin my swing. The ping of the clubface striking the ball is sweet. The flight of the ball is perfect—starting down the right side of the fairway with a slight draw. The ball bounces a few times and comes to a stop in perfect position for my approach shot to the green. The crowd applauds their approval.

From that moment until 5:45 on Sunday afternoon—for just one weekend—every swing is the same—one perfect stroke after another.

From Thursday evening until now, sports reports have encircled the globe. "Stranger Leads Open." "Eighteen Handicapper Wows Golf World." "Who *Is* this Guy?"

As I walk up to the eighteenth green that Sunday afternoon, the crowds are cheering wildly. The guy with the rainbow hair isn't holding up "John 3:16." This weekend his sign just says, "It's a Miracle."

When my putt drops to the bottom of the cup with that familiar rattling sound, I pump my fists and dance around. Now my buddies back home are proud of me. As I walk toward the microphone to receive the Wannamaker Trophy everything goes blank. I wake up. My daydream is over.

Every day—every single day—you and I have an incredible opportunity. This one is even more wonderful than winning the U.S. Open. By God's amazing grace and the presence of the Holy Spirit, we have been infused with the very power of the living God—and *nothing* is too hard for him.

You will receive power when the Holy Spirit comes on you;
And you will be my witnesses in Jerusalem,
and in all Judea and Samaria,
And to the ends of the earth.

ACTS 1:8

It's like having Tiger Wood's drive, Ernie Els' fairway woods, Nick Price's bunker-blasting ability, Jose Maria Olazabal's chipping finesse, and Brad Faxon's putting stroke[2]—only much better. And it's not for just one weekend.

Your arm is powerful.
Your hand is strong.
Your right hand is mighty, O LORD.

PSALM 89:13

The Prayers

A PRAYER *for* YOU

Father in Heaven,

Thank you for the incredible power you provide to your children everyday. Thank you for the glorious plan you have for my family and me. What do you have in mind for today? I want to see what you see. I want the vision of your kingdom to be so firmly planted in my mind that the dream becomes a reality. I want to walk and talk and live with the very power of your Spirit.

I know that nothing is too hard for you, so I ask this in the powerful name of Jesus,

Amen.

A Prayer *for* Your Child

Father in Heaven,

Thank you for the incredible power you have provided for my child. By your amazing grace, please infuse my child with the very spirit that raised Christ from the dead. Make my child alive to the possibilities and the picture of his life lived by your power. Help him to be a winsome witness for you wherever he goes because your strong hand is lifted over him in glorious strength. I ask this because it is what you promised and nothing is too hard for you.

In the powerful name of Jesus Christ,

Amen.

All the resources of the Godhead are at our disposal!

Jonathan Goforth

HANNAH *and* SAMUEL

The Promise

My heart rejoices in the LORD; in the LORD my horn is lifted high.
My mouth boasts over my enemies, for I delight in your deliverance.

1 SAMUEL 2:1

The Picture

"Hi. My name is Robert and I am a recovering impatient."

Although I've never heard of secret meetings held for people who suffer from an addiction to impatience, I could certainly qualify. It seems like I'm always in a hurry.

When Bobbie and I lived in Middle Tennessee, I was constantly haunted by endless miles of two-lane roads complete with double-yellow no-passing stripes. More often than I'd like to admit, I found myself close enough to the slow-moving car in front of me to read even the smallest, mud-crusted bumper sticker.

My battle with patience has often reminded me of the biblical story of Hannah. She might as well be the patron saint of patience. In the account of her journey of faith, we are not told how old Hannah was when she first begged God to give her a child of her own. But we do know that as the years passed, she struggled to be patient and wait for God's answer.

Each year, Elkanah and Hannah went to the temple at Shiloh to worship, and Hannah would spend her time at the altar praying and weeping over her barrenness. Her heart's greatest longing was to have a child.

This bothered Elkanah who became a little jealous of Hannah's desire. All of this was taking his wife's attention away from him.

"Hannah," Elkanah said to her one day, "Why are you weeping? Why don't you eat? Why are your downhearted? Don't I mean more to you than ten sons?"

This story makes me smile every time I read it because the scripture does not record an answer from Hannah to her insecure husband. Her silence seems to be saying, "No, frankly—since you asked—you *don't* mean more to me than ten sons. I want a child!"

Sorry, Elkanah.

One day as Hannah was praying in the temple, Eli the priest spotted her. She was praying silently, but her lips were moving. Eli decided that she must be drunk.

"How long will you keep on getting drunk?" he scolded. "Get rid of your wine."

"Not so, my lord," the misunderstood Hannah replied. "I am a woman who is deeply troubled. I have not been drinking wine or beer; I was pouring out my soul to the LORD. Do not take me for a wicked woman; I have been praying here out of my great anguish and grief."

Seeing her unswerving determination and her great faith, Eli responded. "May the God of Israel grant you what you have asked of him."

This conversation changed everything.

Hannah thanked the priest and left the temple, her heart filled with assurance and hope. Her appetite—and her smile—were restored.

And sure enough, according to Eli's promise, Hannah conceived and gave birth to a boy. She named him Samuel, "because I asked the Lord for him."

As Elkanah prepared for his next visit to the temple, Hannah announced that the baby was too small to travel. "But," she said to her husband, "After the boy is weaned, I will take him to the temple and present him before the Lord, and he will live there always."

So a few years later, when Hannah finished nursing the baby, she brought him to the temple as she had promised. There she presented Samuel to Eli the priest.

"Now I give him to the Lord," she said. "For his whole life he will be given over to the Lord."

It's one thing to take a child to the temple and ask God for his blessing. But this was a one-way trip for Samuel. Hannah literally left her son behind. You would think that giving her son to the Lord would have been a difficult thing for Hannah. Not so. The experience actually filled her with awe.

"My heart rejoices in the Lord," she prayed. "I delight in your deliverance. There is no one holy like the Lord; there is no one besides you; there is no Rock like our God."

As a parent, Hannah understood that there was nothing more wonderful than the act of presenting her child to the Lord. Nowhere would he be more secure.

You may have had to wait for your wife to successfully conceive your children. But even if you didn't, it's certain that you're going to have to be long-suffering while they grow up. Your patience is going to be tested.

Take a deep breath. Don't be in a hurry. Learn the lesson taught by the patient Hannah. Commit your children to the Lord. They'll be safe in his care.

> *The end of a matter is better than its beginning,*
> *and patience is better than pride.*

ECCLESIASTES 7:8

The Prayers

A Prayer *for* You

Father in Heaven,

You are the God of perfect timing. You are never in a hurry. You are trustworthy, and you have a plan. Forgive my impatience. I ask you to slow me down when I have a hard time waiting for your plan. I need your help to enjoy the moments I have with my family. You have blessed me with a new day and you have blessed me with children. Fill me with wisdom so that I may learn to live each moment in obedience to you. Give me joy in every moment. Help me to patiently set an example to my family—to stop, to listen, to enjoy and to pray for each member. I commit my moments and my days to you. Fill them with praise and prayer. I present my child and myself to you.

In the strong name of Jesus,

Amen.

A Prayer *for* Your Child

Father in Heaven,

You are the God of good gifts, all perfectly timed. Thank you for the gift of my child. Thank you for planning every day of her life. There is no safer place for my child than in the center of your will. I bring my child to you. I commit her to you. I leave her in your hands, knowing that you love my child even more than I do. Help my child to learn what it means to stop and listen to your voice. Grant her wisdom far beyond her years. Satisfy her desires in her youth so that she learns how to trust you completely. Let her learn the delight of living in your presence every moment of every day.

In the strong name of Jesus,

Amen.

Patience with others is Love.
Patience with self is Hope.
Patience with God is Faith.

Adel Bestavros

I *a* CWISTIAN

The Promise

Therefore, if anyone is in Christ, He is a new creation;
The old has gone, The new has come!

2 CORINTHIANS 5:17

The Picture

I love new things. Don't you!

I was the third boy in my family so my closet rarely saw brand new things. My dad made a sacrament out of studying the classifieds in the newspaper, so our bicycles, lawnmowers, washing machines, and cars were almost always "second hand."

With this tradition as a backdrop, you can understand how excited I was when I got my first new car—a 1970 green Chevy Malibu. (It was a college graduation present from my penny-wise—but very loving—dad.) I would sit in my car and take deep breaths, filling my lungs with the happy smell. I took pictures of it from every conceivable angle.

I thought that life couldn't get any sweeter—I was wrong.

On September 17, 1971, a nurse handed me something new—something so much better than a new car. "This is baby Melissa," she said. I could hardly breathe. Her ruddy little face was the most wonderful thing I had ever seen. Our first child—I was a daddy.

I thought that life couldn't get any sweeter than that— I was only partially right.[1]

On February 12, 1996, the same little girl I had held 25 years before handed me another little girl, less than a week old. "This is baby Abby," she said. I could hardly breathe. Her ruddy little face was the most wonderful thing I had ever seen. Our first grandchild—I was a granddaddy.

The Bible uses these two images—new things and newborns—to describe the miracle of salvation, the personal experience of God's saving grace.

The verse above talks about new things and this one talks about new birth.

> *To all who received him,*
> *to those who believed in his name,*
> *he gave the right to become children of God—*
> *children born not of natural descent,*
> *nor of human decision or a husband's will,*
> *but born of God.*

JOHN 1:12-13

Your most important job as a dad is to come to Jesus Christ in faith yourself and receive his gift of newness. Jesus called it being "born again."[2] Your second most important job is to bring your children to the Savior.[3] One day a man brought his son to Jesus. The boy was possessed by a demon and his frightened dad did the only thing he could think of. Jesus asked the dad how long the boy had been experiencing these awful convulsions. The father told him that they'd been happening since his son was small.

"If you can do anything," the dad pled, "take pity on us and help us."[4]

"If you can?" Jesus asked. And then he added the most challenging words: "Everything is possible for him who believes."

The sick boy's dad knew what Jesus was saying. His son's healing might depend on the quality of his faith.

"I believe," the dad said confidently. He paused, remembering to whom he was speaking. "Help me overcome my unbelief," a wash of confession sweeping over him.

This dad is exactly like you and me. We *want* to bring our children to Jesus. And we want to believe that he can be trusted with their care. But there is often that shadow of doubt, that vestige of mistrust. Like the dad in the story, we confess our need to be healed of our unbelief. And, true to his word, Jesus touches our children and heals our skepticism.

Not long ago our granddaughter Abby, then almost six years old, was playing with her nearly-four-year-old brother, Luke. It was Christmastime and they were setting up a plastic nativity scene in their playroom. Of course, there were Mary, Joseph, the baby Jesus, a handful of shepherds and some livestock looking on. There were also a couple of Power Ranger action figures and the conductor of Luke's Brio train set.[5]

Missy was busy in the kitchen when Luke walked in with an announcement. "I a Cwistian," he said. Thinking that Luke had said, "I have a question," Missy asked her son what he wanted.

"No," Luke replied. "I a Cwistian!"

An expert at deciphering toddler-eese, now she understood. "Oh, Luke that's wonderful!" Missy said. Luke told her how his big sister had warned him that his action figures may not be Christians[6] and that Jesus didn't need to become a Christian because he was perfect.

"Would you like to ask Jesus into your heart?" Abby asked Luke. "Yes," Luke replied. And so, with the help of his sister, he did. "I copied Abby," Luke said when Missy asked him how he knew what to say.

Bring your children to Jesus. Even if they're very young, they can be made new. Even though they are very small, they can be born again. Just like you.

A little child shall lead them.

ISAIAH 11:6

The Prayers

A PRAYER *for* YOU

Father in Heaven,

You are an amazing God of new things. You created cells and formed life from them. You take a sinful heart like mine and make it clean. Thank you for the gift of newness. Thank you for the gift of salvation and the privilege of being your child. By the power of your cross, the old has gone. By the continuing work of your Holy Spirit, the new has come. I am completely overwhelmed.

I love you with a new and grateful heart.

Amen.

A Prayer *for* Your Child

Father in Heaven,

Today I bring my child to you for the gift of new life that you have given me. Like the dad who brought his son to you for healing, I believe. Help my unbelief to be replaced with the assurance that you love my child even more than I possibly could. I trust you for his salvation and care. I know what you can do in my child's life. With the new life that you breathe into my child, may he lead another as only a child can.

We love you with a new and grateful heart.

Amen.

The first time we we're born, as children, human life is given to

us; and when we accept Jesus as our Savior, it's a new life.

That's what "born again" means.

Jimmy Carter

JACOB *and* JOSEPH

The Promise

May the God before whom my fathers Abraham and Isaac walked,

The God who has been my shepherd all my life to this day,

The Angel who has delivered me from all harm—

May he bless these boys ... and may they increase greatly upon the earth.

GENESIS 48:15-16

The Picture

Joseph loved his father, Jacob. And early in his life, he knew that Jacob loved him as well. Jacob often expressed his love for his "special" son and blessed him often with words and gifts. What could be more wonderful than a father's blessing?

I, too, loved my father. As a small boy I remember feeling the strength of his hands and the tenderness of his heart for God. But my dad grew up in a tradition where words of affirmation from a dad to his son were sparse. I had observed this from visiting his parent's farm and seeing how careful his dad's words were to his son.

"We're glad that you're using your talents for the Lord," they'd say. But because they wanted their son to avoid ego and pride, there was never an "I'm proud of you" or "Great job, son!"

Unlike Joseph, my dad grew up never hearing words of direct affirmation from his dad.

In 1986, as my dad's father was nearing the end of his life, I went to visit him. Sitting on the edge of his bed, I told him how much I loved him and how thankful I was for the godly legacy he was leaving behind. At this, my grandfather lifted his hand to my shoulder and spontaneously began to pray a blessing on my children and me. I was stunned at this expression of tenderness.

As soon as I had a chance, I told my dad of my conversation with his father and of his words of blessing. He told me that he had never heard words like these from his dad. So I decided to begin speaking words of blessing to my father. And for the final fifteen years of my dad's life, I passed my grandfather's words on to him.

"I'm proud of you, Dad," I would say when I'd face discouragement and remembered how courageous he was throughout his life. "I'm proud of you, Dad," I would say when someone told me how my father had impacted their life or when I was reminded how he had impacted mine. Over and over again, I told my dad that I was thankful for his integrity and the consistency of his life. I knew that he loved hearing these words because my siblings and I began to hear him say these words back to us. Even his grandchildren heard their Papa tell them how proud he was of them. What could be more wonderful than a father's—or a grandfather's—blessing?

In a fit of jealousy, Joseph's ten older brothers sold Joseph—then only a teenager—to the Midianites for twenty shekels of silver. These nomads were traveling through Canaan toward Egypt when Joseph's hateful brothers traded him into slavery. Then they told Jacob that Joseph was dead, killed by wild animals.

For almost twenty years Jacob thought his son was dead. But he wasn't. When they finally met again, Joseph—now an Egyptian governor—and Jacob held onto each other and wept. Nothing in Jacob's life had replaced his love for his son. And nothing in Joseph's life had taken the place of his father's blessing.

Then Joseph brought his two young boys, Manasseh and Ephraim, to meet their grandfather. "These are the sons God has given me here," he said.

Crawling up on their grandfather's lap, Jacob kissed the boys and embraced them. "I never expected to see your face again," he told Joseph, "and now God has allowed me to see your children, too."

Joseph and his sons knelt before Jacob as he lifted his voice and spoke the words of promise you read today.

What could be more wonderful than a father's blessing? Your children need your blessing, too. They need to hear affirming words like, "I'm proud of you" and "You are special to me." Don't neglect this important responsibility. Even though they hear the words from others, never will they have a greater impact than when they come from your lips.

Like Joseph, your children may attain greatness. They may become independent, accomplished individuals who seem to lack nothing. But nothing can take the place of those words of blessing they receive from you—nothing at all.

Jesus took the children in his arms,
placed his hands on each of them, and blessed them.

MARK 10:16

The Prayers

A PRAYER *for* YOU

Father in Heaven,

You are the God of promise and blessing. Thank you for your Word that promises me your blessings. I read your tender expressions of divine approval and feel your hand lifted over me in love. I pray for my child as I claim these same blessings in her life. I speak blessings over her as you do over me. I am not capable of loving my family as I should. I ask for wisdom to think and speak the words that will surround my child with the unconditional love you provide. I recognize the power of the blessing my love and words can have on the lives of every one of my family members. With the instructions from your Word, I ask you to carry these blessings far into my tomorrows.

In the name and power of Jesus,

Amen.

A Prayer *for* Your Child

Father in Heaven,

You are the God of promise and blessing. Thank you for the gift of my child. May the mind of Christ live in him from day to day. May the love of Jesus fill him and the peace of Jesus rule his heart. May your beauty rest upon him. With your strength, may my child run the race before him. May he look steadily into your truth. As you have been with me, so be with my child in every way. May he be so blessed that his life is an outpouring of your love to others. And may he walk before you forever in godliness and integrity. Bless and keep my child. Into your gracious care I commit his life.

In the name and power of Jesus,

Amen.

JUST WALK
BEHIND *the* PLOW

The Promise

Sow for yourself righteousness, reap the fruit of unfailing love,
and break up your unplowed ground;
for it is time to seek the LORD,
until he comes and showers righteousness on you.

HOSEA 10:12

The Picture

My dad grew up on Mount Joy,[1] Lancaster County, Pennsylvania farm. Although we don't actually have a photograph of this, one of my favorite mental "pictures" of my dad is plowing huge fields as a boy, walking behind a single mule—the blade of the plow slicing through the stubborn ground.

Hour upon hour of guiding the plow through the stubborn soil gave Samuel Wolgemuth an opportunity to dream.

One of his dreams was to take the message of God's grace to the world—to plow through the lostness of men's hearts and sprinkle the seeds of healing and hope. He wanted to be a missionary.

I was five years old when his first assignment took our family of six to Tokyo, Japan. At 38 and 36, my dad and mother placed almost all of their earthly possessions on the front yard and sold them. Then they moved my sister, two brothers, and me to the Orient.

These were the days when "mission work" meant one thing—sending Americans to different parts of the world. My dad's experience caused him to see the fallacy of that. "Mission work should be local," he'd say, "then the message can be delivered within the context of the people's culture—and foreign missionaries don't have to come and go."

In 1986, my dad, the Pennsylvania farm boy, presided over the first World

Council of Youth for Christ, International. In the meeting were 51 national leaders, all missionaries to their *own* countries. This was a landmark moment in the history of world missions. That plow was very sharp.

As he walked behind the plow, my dad also dreamed of getting married to Grace Dourte, the elegant brunette from Manheim, just a few miles from Mount Joy. And he dreamed of raising a family—boys and girls whose hearts would become tender and receptive to God's voice. He knew that was the most important thing of all.

When we laid my dad to rest on February 11, 2002, his six children and their spouses were standing by his grave. Twenty grandchildren and thirteen great grandchildren were also there. Our dad's work, message, and disciplined example had guided the plow through the soil of lives and the seeds of God's grace were taking root. That plow was very sharp.

Regardless of our vocations, you and I are farmers walking behind a plow. The blade is God's gift of faith, the ground is our family, and the seed is God's Word.

As dads our call is to keep the plow sharp by the example of our own faith. We must expose our children to Christian activities, like Bible reading, prayer at meals and bedtime, church membership, Christian music, and conversations about God's love. And we must guide the plow with a life that's godly, disciplined and consistent.

One day, Jesus told his followers a story taken from Mark, chapter 4 about a farmer scattering seed. Some fell along the path, and the birds came and ate it up.

Some fell on rocky places, where it did not have much soil. It sprang up quickly...but when the sun came up...it withered because it had no root. Other seed fell among the thorns, which grew up and choked the plants. Still other seed fell on good soil. It came up, grew and produced a crop, multiplying thirty, sixty or even a hundred times.[2]

Jesus went on to explain that the seed was the word of God and the places where the seed landed were people's hearts. Hard ground provided dinner for birds. Rocky ground made for a temporary harvest. Thorny ground gave the weeds power over the seed. Good ground produced good fruit.

What Jesus could have added was that it was the farmer's job to make sure the seed fell on good soil. In fact, the farmer could have turned any of the soils into productive dirt if he had sharpened his plow and guided it through the ground.

My dad was a humble man. He was not a great scholar or a brilliant orator. But he learned how to be a faithful farmer and he walked behind the plow.

As for you, brothers,

Never tire of doing what is right.

2 THESSALONIANS 3:13

And that's all you and I need to do—just walk behind the plow.

Let us not become weary in doing good,
for at the proper time we will reap a harvest,
if we do not give up.

The Prayers

A PRAYER *for* YOU

Father in Heaven,

You are the Mighty God who produces a bountiful harvest with the seed of your Word. I want my life to bear the fruits of love, joy, peace, patience, kindness, goodness, faithfulness, gentleness and self-control. I need the good soil of your Spirit to produce these things in me. I give you permission to sharpen the plow and slice through anything in my life that keeps your message from taking root. I ask you to plow up any stubborn ground in my heart. As I take on the role of being a farmer in my own household, give me the steady reassurance that your hand is on the plow with mine. Thank you for your promises that assure my productivity. I want my family to bear such beautiful fruit that our friends and neighbors will be generously fed by its bounty.

In the strong name of Jesus,

Amen

A PRAYER *for* YOUR CHILD

Father in Heaven,

Thank you for making my child's heart the tender soil where your Word can be planted. Thank for your Spirit and the promise that your Word will not return without success. Today, may the seeds of love, joy, peace, patience, kindness, goodness, faithfulness, gentleness and self-control take root in my child. As I stand behind the plow, guide the sharpened blade of discipline and love through the rich soil of his life. Produce a bountiful harvest so others may be nourished by my child's life.

In the strong name of Jesus,

Amen

The renewal of our natures is a work of great importance.
It is not to be done in a day. We have not only a new home
to build up, but an old one to pull down.

GEORGE WHITEFIELD

No Tatoos on
Their Hearts

The Promise

The LORD does not look at the things man looks at.

Man looks at the outward appearance,

But the LORD looks at the heart.

1 SAMUEL 16:7

The Picture

Until Southwest Airlines came along, I had never flown backwards.

You know what I'm talking about, don't you? The first row on Southwest jets faces the back of the plane and, actually, I don't mind sitting there. It can be an interesting experience, looking into the faces of all your fellow passengers.

Early one morning, I was flying backwards on Southwest from Nashville to Chicago. The moment I sat down I looked at the row of folks sitting straight across from me. The person directly opposite my seat was a young man, probably 19 or 20 years old.

His t-shirt had a sequence of illustrations on it, depicting a couple having sex. You can imagine the obscene captions under each of the drawings. I looked at his face. There were rings or studs everywhere . . . in his nose, his eyebrow, his tongue, and four or five on each of his ears. Grotesque tattoos covered his arms and neck.

At that moment, I made a determination about the young man whose knees were literally against mine. This was a lost and very naughty boy.

Once the flight attendant announced that "approved electronic devices may now be used," I pulled out my laptop computer and began to answer a stack of e-mail. Every once in a while I'd glance up. The moment I did, the young man would look away. *He's staring at me*, I thought to myself.

Doesn't he have something else to do?

I went back to my work.

About 30 minutes into the flight, something nudged me. No, that's wrong. Someone nudged me and whispered in my ear. Talk to him, a Voice said.

You've got to be kidding me, I responded. I've got work to do … and besides …

But the Voice wasn't listening. *Talk to him*, it repeated.

I looked up from composing a memo to one of my clients. "Good morning," I said, looking directly into his face. "You headed home?"

The expression on his face said it all. A button-down guy is talking to me. This guy's old enough to be my dad. What in the world does he want?

"Huh?" the young man answered, looking around to see if I may have said good morning to someone else.

"Are you headed home to Chicago or do you live in Nashville?" I repeated.

"Oh … uh, I'm goin' home," he stammered, a thin smile reluctantly forming on his face.

"Chicago's a great town," I replied. "I live in Nashville now, but Chicago will always be my home. It's a great place to live."

"Yeah," he said. "It's a good place all right."

I closed the lid to my laptop and it gave me an I'm-going-to-sleep beep. The memos could wait.

This began one of the most important conversations of my life. The young man's name was Jason. He had run away from home at 16. Hitchhiking to the West Coast with a duffel bag and his guitar, he had "gotten involved in some pretty wild stuff." I could only imagine.

Someone had told Jason to take his guitar and go to Nashville. But soon he discovered that there were better musicians waiting tables than he'd ever hope to be. Jason found a job washing dishes. Then two weeks ago, his parents called and invited him to come home. It had been four years since he had seen them—and four years since they had seen him!

I was delighted with Jason's bright mind and his quick wit. I was also taken with the tenderness of his voice and his genuine hope in the reunion with his mother and his dad. His eyes welled up with tears as he talked about being with his family again. Until the wheels screeched our welcome to Midway, we talked non-stop.

"Shame" would be a perfect word to describe how I felt as I walked down the concourse to the rental car counter. When I had first looked at Jason, he might as well have had one more tattoo across his forehead: "Loser." Now I realized that the moniker belonged to me.

When the Israelites first met Saul, they were overwhelmed by his physique, his good looks, and his charm. He would have been the perfect traveling companion on any flight. So they crowned him as their king.

But, as it turned out, Saul was a self-absorbed, arrogant and very disobedient man—a great disappointment to everyone, especially to a holy God. So the Lord sent a message to the prophet Samuel. "Don't be fooled," God said. "You looked on the outside of the man, but I looked into his heart."

As your children grow up, they're going to be bringing their friends to your house. Some of these kids will look like Saul. You'll be impressed. And some of them will look like Jason. You'll take a deep breath.

That conversation to Chicago was one of the most important of my life. It wasn't only my seat that was backwards. I believe that God was telling me, "Look at the boy's heart," he said. There are no tattoos there." I'm sorry, Jason. Thank you, Lord.

Accept him whose faith is weak,

without passing judgment on disputable matters.

Romans 14:1

The Prayers

A PRAYER *for* YOU

Father in Heaven,

You are holy and just. You look straight into our hearts. There are times that I look down on others because they have a different style than I'm comfortable with. I don't see my own sinfulness. I like to look good and cover up what's really in my heart. Forgive me for thinking I am better than someone else. I need you to give me your eyes of love for broken and hurting people. When I'm impressed by someone's good looks or clothing, remind me that you look at the thoughts and intentions of hearts. Starting right now, let my attitude be like yours. You are God and yet you make yourself available to sinful people, no matter what we look like on the outside. I am now available to be your loving eyes and kind voice to whoever needs your touch.

Through your power alone,

Amen.

A Prayer *for* Your Child

Father in Heaven,

Please give my child a discerning heart. Help her to be wise and prudent as she chooses her friends. Give her a loving heart, willing to reach out to others wherever and whenever you provide her with opportunities.

In the strong name of Jesus,

Amen.

PROPHET, PRIEST and KING

The Promise

*Your word is a lamp to my feet
and a light to my path, O Lord.*

PSALM 119:105

The Picture

Imagine this: You're on a commuter train from your home into the city and you're about to open the newspaper. You've been doing this for years. It's your daily routine.

Just before you snap open Section A, you notice a stranger sitting next to you. You turn and say an insincere "good morning." Unfortunately, he doesn't catch the hypocrisy of your greeting and thinks you actually want to talk.

The next few frustrating minutes are filled with comments about the weather, and the loss the home team took in the game last night and—worst of all—questions. "What's your business?" he inevitably asks. You do your very best to slough off the question with a quick answer. He's not satisfied.

"Do you have a business card?" he asks.

"Sure," you say as you reach into the front pocket of your briefcase. You hand him a card, hoping this will, at least temporarily, assuage his curiosity.

He thanks you and reads each word on the card—out loud! Your name, your address, your zip code, your phone number, your fax number, and your cell phone number. *Who is this guy?* you wonder.

He's about to read your title when he stops. You know that he's completely dumbfounded by it. But, like he did with the other information on the card, he proceeds to read out loud, though more slowly and, unfortunately, more loudly.

"Prophet, Priest, and King."

Without lifting your head, your eyes scan the rail car. Your suspicion is confirmed. People—lots of them—are listening to every word.

Until you reach your destination, your newspaper lies quietly on your lap. You have some explaining to do. Your seatmate and a few of his friends are eager to hear what you have to say. It goes something like this.

In his letter to the people in Ephesus, chapter 6, verse 4, the Apostle Paul gave fathers a job description. "Do not exasperate your children," he wrote. "Instead, bring them up in the training and instruction of the Lord."

One day, a few years ago, you decided to take these words seriously. In your research, you discovered some very interesting things about the people who God commissioned to be responsible for "the training and instruction of the Lord." You had narrowed this down to three roles: prophet, priest, and king.

In the Old Testament, *prophets* were commissioned to stand before the people, facing them. Sometimes they would open their remarks with, "Thus says the Lord." But even if they didn't use these words, it was *always* what they were doing—speaking on behalf of the Lord to his people.

And when the people heard the prophet's words, they knew that, like it or not, he was speaking God's truth.

Most of the priests were actually born into their calling. They were descendents of Levi, one of Jacob's sons. They were the ones who conducted the meetings that ushered the people into the Lord's presence. When they stood in front of the assemblies, they often faced the altar with their backs to the congregations. Their job was to plead the people's case before the living God. Men, women, and children would hear the priests beseech Jehovah for protection, for righteousness, for mercy, and for pardon on their behalf.

The priest even had the names of the twelve tribes of Israel engraved on his breastplate to remind everyone that he was standing in their place.[1]

Of the three men, the kings were the most powerful. The example of their personal lives set the tone for the entire nation. As the king was obedient to the voice of God, the nation prospered. And when the king sinned, the nation suffered.

Kings led their people into plenty or want, into victory or defeat, by their own conduct.

Every Christian dad bears the duty of godly training and instruction for his family. Like a prophet, it's his job to know God's word and be so tuned to his voice that he can speak God's truth. Like a priest, he must plead his children's case before God, asking for blessing, protection, guidance, and forgiveness. And like a noble king, he sets the tone in his home by his own godly example.

By the time the train reaches your stop, many of the people in the car have listened to everything you've said. As you step onto the platform, you breathe a prayer of thanks for your inquisitive neighbor. The commute today was a good reminder of who you are—prophet, priest, and king—to your children.

> *You will be called priests of the LORD.*
> *You will be named workers for our God.*
>
> ISAIAH 61:6 NIRV

The Prayers

A PRAYER *for* YOU

Father in Heaven,

Thank you for Jesus who pleads my case before your Holy throne. Because of his righteousness, he puts me in a place of mercy before you. The task of being prophet, priest, and king for my own family overwhelms me. But I know that when you call me to do something, you always give me your power with which to accomplish it. Thank you for the privilege of facing my family to speak the words you give to me. Thank you for allowing me to live in your presence as I face the altar of your grace on behalf of my family. Help me to be an example of a man who obeys you daily. Today, help me to set the tone in my home by taking the full responsibility to be prophet, priest and king.

In the power of Jesus' name,

Amen.

A PRAYER *for* YOUR CHILD

Here I stand in your Holy presence with the name of my child engraved on my heart. Look at each one. I plead for your mercy, for your protection, and for your guidance for my child. Only you can accomplish your purposes for my child. He needs your holy and immediate presence to obey you. Help him to listen to your voice today. May he hear your voice when he hears mine. May the words of my mouth and the meditations of my heart lead him in the way of righteousness.

In the name of our prophet, priest and king: Jesus,

Amen.

What a father says to his children
is not heard by the world,
but it will be heard by posterity.

JEAN PAUL RICHTER

PUT *it in* WRITING

The Promise

Like cold water to a weary soul
Is good news from a distant land.

PROVERBS 25:25

The Picture

Several years ago I had a conversation with a very close friend. The subject of our conversation was the value of handwritten notes—thank you notes, get well notes, congratulatory notes, and just plain I'm-thinking-of-you notes.

I told him how a few years before I had received a handwritten note from my good friend, Billy Webb. We had just had lunch together and Billy dropped me a note on a single card with his name engraved at the top: "WILLIAM V.B. WEBB". The note was only a few sentences: "Robert—Thanks for lunch today. I'm so lucky to have a good friend like you. Have a terrific rest of the week. You're the best. Your friend, Billy."

I remember thinking to myself as I slipped the card back into the envelope—Wow, I can do this. So I became a note writer.

Making contact with a stationery supplier in Nashville, where we lived, I ordered a couple hundred cards with my name printed at the top, and I use them all the time.

One day, I saw my wife's car in the grocery store parking lot. I drove over to it, got a business card out of my wallet, wrote "I Love You" on the back and slipped it under her windshield wiper.

For years, this card was taped to the back of the kitchen cabinet where we keep coffee mugs—the one she used most in the kitchen. Without meaning to, Bobbie was telling me how important handwritten notes were.

Our children also let me know how important handwritten notes were. When they were in grade school, Bobbie packed their lunch every day. The last thing to go into the little brown bag was a paper napkin. And before she slipped the napkin into the bag, she'd write something on it: "Julie: I hope you're having a wonderful day. Don't forget how much I love you. Mom." Sometimes she'd ask me to write the napkin-note: "Missy: You're the best. I love you. Dad."

Our children loved these notes. "What did your mom say today?" their friends would chide as they unpacked their lunches. Our kids would proudly read their note.[1]

But it wasn't until the note from Billy Webb that I got the message about getting into the habit of doing handwritten notes. This time the message stuck. Actually, it shouldn't have taken Billy Webb to remind me of the value of notes. Solomon likened news from afar to "cold water to a weary soul."

It's probably been fifteen years since I placed my first order for note cards. And what I've discovered is that these cards are contagious. Just like the day when I "caught the bug" from Billy, others have caught it from me. I have a bulging file in my office credenza called "Important Notes." I've emptied it several times over the years and it needs it again. As you might guess, my favorites are the ones from my wife and kids and grandkids.

A colleague and I had a conversation about handwritten notes. She asked me if I thought an e-mail note was the same as a handwritten note. I thought about it for a while and said, "I don't think so." We talked about it some more and she agreed. There's nothing quite as authentic as having a person's words written out in their own hand. (Autograph hounds wouldn't be satisfied with an e-mail signature from their favorite sport's hero, would they? See what I mean?)

The other day, I got to thinking about another great example of handwritten notes. When it came time for God to send us a special message, he sent Jesus. Like a hand in a glove, God slipped himself into a human body that could know "physical pain, hunger, thirst, winter's chill, summer's heat, exhaustion, and poverty."[2] Jesus became the most important handwritten message in history. "I love you," a holy God was saying to lost people. This note changed everything.

Have you written a note lately? Give it a try. Write to your children and tell them how much you love them and how much God loves them. Tell them how delighted you are to be their father. Tell them you are praying for them. See what happens.

The next thing most like living one's life over again
seems to be a recollection of that life, and to make that recollection
as durable as possible by putting it down in writing.

BENJAMIN FRANKLIN

The art of art, the glory of expression
and the sunshine of the light of letters, is simplicity.

WALT WHITMAN

Go now, write it on a tablet for them,
inscribe it on a scroll,
that for the days to come
it may be an everlasting witness.

ISAIAH 30:8

May our Lord Jesus Christ himself and God our Father,
who loved us and by his grace gave us eternal encouragement
and good hope, encourage your hearts
and strengthen you in every good deed and word.

2 THESSALONIANS 2:16–17

The Prayers

A PRAYER *for* YOU

Father in Heaven,

Thank you for sending Jesus as the most amazing handwritten note in history. Thank you that the message you wrote with his life is "I love you." Thank you for the written word of Scripture that daily encourages me and inspires me. Today, help me to be aware of who needs a handwritten note from me. I commit to take a few minutes to write a note of encouragement to someone this week. Please use my pen to speak love and inspiration into the lives of my family and friends and coworkers. I want to be like you and change someone's day by giving a gift of encouraging words.

In the power of your word,

Amen

A Prayer *for* Your Child

Father in Heaven,

Thank you for sending a love note to my child in the form of a Savior. Today, I ask that you encourage my child with the power of words. Your word is a light for her path and a lamp for her feet. As she receives a handwritten note from me, let her get hooked on the idea of sharing good words with others. Let her feel my love and know that I'm thinking of her. Bless her with the confidence that she is loved. With that encouragement, help her to be a giver of blessings to our family and her friends.

With the power of your word,

Amen.

Encouragement is oxygen to the soul.

Author Unknown

SPEAKING *the* POSSIBLE

The Promise

When the angel of the LORD appeared to Gideon he said,

"The LORD is with you, mighty warrior."

The Picture

It happened a lot when our daughters were small.

Our family would be somewhere—a restaurant, church, in an airport or shopping mall—and we'd see a little girl about the same age. Right away we'd notice something striking about this child: crystal-blue eyes or dancing, curly blonde hair.

But no matter how adorable the child might be, Bobbie and I kept our mouths shut.

Our daughters were born with brown eyes, a gift from their dad. And they were born with straight light brown hair, a gift from their mother. What if we had said, "Oh, look at that girl over there … and would you look at those beautiful blue eyes and pretty blonde hair?"

What would Missy and Julie have thought? They had no control over the color of their eyes or the texture of their hair. But their dad or mother had just placed a high price on something they could do nothing about. We would have spoken an impossibility, a terribly frustrating experience for anyone, especially a child.

Instead, we looked for things in other children that our daughters *could* achieve. "Did you notice how that girl spoke to her mother? She was so polite." "Isn't it fun to meet a boy who has such good manners?"

At that moment, our daughters understood two things:

1) their parents admired good manners, and

2) this is something they can do, too.

My wife and I were speaking the possible into our children's souls. *We can't have blue eyes but we can have good manners*, they might have been thinking to themselves.

There's a story way back in the Old Testament about a man named Gideon. A farmer by trade, the last thing Gideon considered himself to be was a brave soldier or a great military strategist. In fact, when we meet him, he seems to be hiding. He was certainly a poor candidate for any kind of leadership.

But the nation of Israel was in trouble. The Midianites and the Amalekites had besieged their land and God was looking for a leader for his people.

"The Lord is with you," the angel said to Gideon. And then he added, "Mighty warrior." God had spoken the possible.

Such a thing had never occurred to Gideon. In fact, he argued with God. "My clan is weak, and I'm the least in my family."

But the Lord answered, "I will be with you, and you will strike down all the Midianites."

The account of Gideon's defeat of the Midianite army is one of the great battle stories in the Bible. With only 300 men, he obliterated an enemy boasting 100 thousand troops. God had spoken the possible into Gideon's soul. And in response Gideon rose to the occasion, accomplishing the task God had assigned to him.

Mighty warrior? Gideon must have said to himself after God's repeated reassurances. *I can do that.*

And so he did.

It would be impossible to measure the influence you wield as a dad. Your words are weighty and powerful. You can help your children picture themselves doing great things. You have the power to strengthen their resolve to live a godly life. You can be a dad who sets his children on the path to success.

Being a godly father is like being a great coach. As you watch your children grow, you assess their strengths. You speak the possible into those strengths. You avoid frustrating them with what they'll never achieve. And then you cheer like crazy from the sidelines.

Like Gideon, your children may be looking for someone who believes in them, someone with a vision of what they could really become. What you have to do is speak the possible. They're waiting to hear good words from you.

Do not use harmful words,
but only helpful words,
the kind that build up
and provide what is needed,
so that what you say
will do good to those who hear you.

EPHESIANS 4:29 GNT

The Prayers

A PRAYER *for* YOU

Father in Heaven,

You are a strong and mighty God. You know how to build confidence in your children. I want you to assess my strengths and assure me of who I am in you. I need your courage to be the man of character that you want me to be. If you are with me, I can be a great coach to my child. With words of affirmation and correction, I can cheer him on to be a brave and gallant leader in your kingdom. Speak affirmation to my soul. Today I commit to confidently and courageously lead my family with words of affirmation.

In the strong name of Jesus,

Amen.

A Prayer *for* Your Child

Father in Heaven,

You are a mighty God of miracles. I know you are looking for leaders for your kingdom work on earth. My child is just the brave and courageous one you want. As I speak "mighty warrior" into the ears of my child, I ask that you speak strength into his heart. May he grasp the vision of what he can truly become. Help my child to believe in the miracle of your power and bravely become the capable recruit you can use.

This I pray for my child and for your glory,

Amen.

Cold words freeze people, and hot words scorch them, and
bitter words make them bitter, and wrathful words
make them wrathful. Kind words also produce their image
on men's souls and a beautiful image it is.

Blaise Pascal

The BIRDS and the BEES

The Promise

He who began a good work in you
Will carry it on to completion
Until the day of Christ Jesus.

PHILIPPIANS 1:6

The Picture

It happens every year—like clockwork. On October 23, thousands of swallows leave their mud nests tucked away in the nooks and crevices of the old mission at San Juan Capistrano and fly away for the winter. That alone wouldn't make the news, except that these little birds are on a 30-day journey that will take them to Goya, Argentina, 7,500 miles away.[1]

Fifteen hours a day, without stopping for food or water, these tiny birds make their way south at an altitude of almost seven thousand feet. At that height, they're able to take advantage of prevailing tail winds and avoid larger predatory birds who may be looking for an airborne snack.

Then, on March 19, the birds return to their summer home in California. So precise is their itinerary that townspeople schedule celebrations months in advance. And every spring, right on time, the swallows return.

Who tells these little creatures when to leave? Who sets the direction of their journey or tells them how to prepare?

Not long ago, Bobbie and I were out for an early evening walk in our neighborhood. We stopped in front of the Jones' house. Todd and Joanna were standing on the street, talking to a few other neighbors. Kids on bicycles and skateboards swirled among the adults like bees among the blossoms. Actually, that's exactly what we talked about that night—honeybees.

Todd is in the produce-shipping business—mostly watermelons. He told us how sophisticated and high-tech the farming world is becoming. "It used to be that we'd load huge semi-trailers with melons and pack them with straw for protection," Todd told us. "Once they arrived at their destinations, we'd take them out and put them in huge cardboard boxes on pallets for distribution to grocery stores."

That's the way it used to be.

Now they have large collapsible plastic boxes with built-in pallets. These crates are also equipped with electronic GPS devices that keep track of their exact locations. People at the distribution centers, sitting in front of computer screens, can watch the movements of the watermelon crates anywhere in the world. I got so excited about Todd's story, reveling in how technologically brilliant our world has become.

Because my own lineage is filled with farmers, I asked about the farms across Florida and into the north that grow the watermelons. As an aside, Todd mentioned beehives.

"Beehives?" I asked.

Todd was taken back by the surprised—and as it turned out, the ignorant—tone of my city-boy voice.

"Yes, beehives," he said. "For every acre of watermelons our farmers plant, we have to set one hive of bees. We can have pristine plants in the ground, we can irrigate and fertilize them perfectly. But, if there are no bees, there's no fruit. None."

Satellite tracked pallets would stay folded and empty. Chrome-piped, exhaust-belching eighteen wheelers would sit quietly. Farmers and picnickers would go hungry—if it weren't for these little creatures. My wife and I were amazed by the wonder of it all.

Who tells these bees how to build their hives with geometric precision? Who shows them how to fly from flower to flower, accidentally dropping pollen as they make their honey? Who speaks to them?

Your child's life is a journey, more perilous than the swallows headed for Argentina. It's a complex sequence of twists and turns—friends and educational choices, finding spouses, selecting careers, raising families of their own—more intricate than bees pollinating watermelon blossoms.

As influential as you and I think we are in our children's lives, most of the time they're on their own.

Who is going to help them on their journey? How will they know what provisions to take along? How will they know where they should go? Who will speak to them?

This is what the LORD says—
Your Redeemer, the Holy One of Israel:
"I am the LORD your God,
Who teaches you what is best for you,
Who directs you in the way you should go."

ISAIAH 48:17

The Prayers

A PRAYER *for* YOU

Father in Heaven,

You are Creator of the universe. I am amazed at the intricacy and power of your design. I worship you as I look at what you have made. Thank you for providing a plan for my journey. And to think that you thought it up before the foundations of the earth were formed! I want to listen to your nudging and follow your directions. What do you have in mind today for my family and me? I am listening. And, like the birds flying in formation, I will follow your lead.

In the powerful name of Jesus Christ,

Amen.

A Prayer *for* Your Child

Father in Heaven,

You are the God of Creation. You formed my child in her mother's womb. You planned every day of her life before the foundations of the world. Today, let my child sense the miracle of your creation. Let her sense the gentle presence of your Spirit guiding her in the direction that you have chosen. Make clear the path of preparation that she needs to follow. Thank you for never losing track of exactly where my child is at every moment. Give her wisdom and instruction to stay on course.

In the powerful and strong name of Jesus,

Amen.

I am satisfied that when the Almighty wants me to do or not to do any particular thing, he finds a way of letting me know.

ABRAHAM LINCOLN

The DOOR

The Promise

I know your deeds.

See, I have placed before you an open door that no one can shut.

I know that you have little strength,

Yet you have kept My word and have not denied My name.

REVELATION 3:8

The Picture

The next time you're visiting your neighborhood home improvement center, go to the customer service counter and ask to speak with "someone who really knows doors."

BEEP: SOMEONE WHO REALLY KNOWS DOORS DIAL 344. SOMEONE WHO REALLY KNOWS DOORS DIAL 344. (I'm not sure why, but they usually repeat these messages. Maybe they have sleeping teenagers at home.)

In a few minutes a nice-looking middle-aged man walks up to you, wearing a bright orange bib. His name is clearly marked: Clyde. You put out your hand and introduce yourself. "I'm Clyde," he replies.

"I understand that you're the door expert here," you say.

Clyde nods. "I sure am."

"Good," you say, smiling. "I have a door question for you."

"Shoot."

"What do you have in Christian doors?"

Clyde blinks a couple times and lifts his hand to scratch his head. "Christian doors?" he says quizzically.

"Yes, Christian doors," you repeat.

"Just a minute," Clyde says, his furrowed brow telling the story. "Let me check the computer." It's back to door school for Clyde.

If Clyde really knew his stuff about doors, he would have known about Christian doors. In colonial America, this name was given to "six-panel doors." And the chances are good that your house is full of them.

The next time you have a chance, stand in front of one of these doors and you'll see how they got their name. The center portion of the top two thirds forms a perfect cross. The lower third looks like the pages of an open book—in this case, an open Bible.

What the early American settlers knew was something that you and I also know: the Bible has a lot to say about doors. And they also knew that when your house is full of Christian doors, they tell a story every time you open one of them.

In Egypt, God told the Jews to take the blood of a lamb and paint it on the doorframes to protect their firstborn from death.[1] This was the first Passover and the message was clear; the door to your house protects your family.

Later, God commanded parents to take his law and write it on the doorposts of their homes and on their gates.[2] The door to your house identifies you as a truth-keeper and locks faithfulness inside.

Jesus continues the metaphor by warning families that when we reject him, the door to his kingdom can be shut so tightly that no matter how much we knock, the door will not be opened.[3] There's nothing we can do on our own to get in.

And he completes the picture by making a stunning claim in John 10:9. "I am the door," Jesus said. "If anyone enters by me, he shall go in and out and find pasture"(KJV).

In the last book of the Bible, the Apostle John adds an interesting wrinkle to this Bible story about doors. To a group of people who were careless about their faith, he called their complacency a door and invited them to open it to him.[4]

Doors protect from danger, they lock in God's holiness, and because of Jesus, they provide a means of rescue. Doors also give us a chance to invite the Savior into our homes as a welcomed guest.

These are all wonderful descriptions of the door to your home. And you're holding the key. If you have never done this, open you own heart's door and invite Jesus Christ in. Then, from your own experience of God's grace, you can begin to pray that your children will also answer the door and invite him into their lives. Doing this is the greatest privilege you will ever have in your role as a father. Take to heart the words of Jesus:

Here I am!
I stand at the door and knock.
If any of you hears my voice and opens the door,
I will come in and eat with you.
And you will eat with me.

REVELATION 3:20, NIRV

The next time you see Clyde, please let him know.

The Prayers

A Prayer *for* You

Father in Heaven,

You are the door of salvation. I open the door to you, Lord Jesus—the door to my heart and the door to my home. Thank you for your Word that is the open book of truth. Thank you for standing at the door and welcoming me in as your guest. Forgive me for allowing sin to enter my home and closing you out. I come knocking at the door, asking you to rescue my family and me. Remind me to think of Truth every time I see a six-panel door. For the protection of my family, I want your Word written on the doorposts of my heart and my home. I ask you to fill my life and my family with your loving and healing presence. You are welcome here.

This I pray in Jesus' name,

Amen.

A Prayer *for* Your Child

Father in Heaven,

You are the door of salvation for my child. I ask you to lovingly and relentlessly knock on the door to his heart. Thank you for your covenant promises to my child. Thank you for the truth of the open book of your Word and the protection it provides for my child. With the sure sign of salvation painted over the doorpost of his heart, protect him from harm. Lock in your holiness as he spends time in your presence. Thank you for filling my child with your love, protection, and healing power. You are the only one who can rescue him. You are the way, the truth and the life.

I pray these things in the strong name of Jesus, the Door,

Amen.

Salvation means the incoming into human nature of the great characteristics that belong to God.

Oswald Chambers

TURN *it* OFF, HAVE *a* TALK

The Promise

When Jesus was at the table with them,
He took bread, gave thanks, broke it and began to give it to them.
Then their eyes were opened and they recognized him,
and he disappeared from their sight.
They asked each other, "Were not our hearts burning within us
while he talked with us on the road?"

Luke 24:30–32

The Picture

It's one of my favorite stories in the Bible. Two men—Cleopas and his friend—were walking from Jerusalem to the town of Emmaus. It was Easter Sunday and these followers of Jesus had left the city after hearing that Jesus' tomb had been found empty. They were very sad because, as far as they knew, his body had been stolen.

As they walked along, they were talking earnestly about all the incredible things that had happened in the past few days. Suddenly a stranger was walking along with them. He asked what they were discussing. They looked at the stranger in disbelief. They couldn't believe he hadn't heard about Jesus being crucified and then his body disappearing from the tomb.

When they were finished telling their story, Jesus explained how all the prophecies had been fulfilled through his life. But they still didn't know who he was.

Because it was late in the day when they arrived at Emmaus, the men invited Jesus to join them for dinner and spend the night. He agreed. At the table, Jesus offered a prayer, broke the bread, and handed it to them. At that very moment their eyes were opened and they recognized Jesus for who he really was.[1]

The end result of their focused conversation along the road was the gift of finally seeing Jesus. But I wonder if that type of visit could have taken place in the culture in which we now live.

Over the past few years, Bobbie and I have noticed how electronic gadgetry—as wonderful as it is—has become a serious threat to the art of conversation.

We've visited homes where the television is never turned off. Even during meals, a ballgame, talk show or the evening news blares from the corner set. When we lived in Tennessee, we used to see a couple on their regular walking route, both wearing Walkmans! You've probably seen kids wearing these in the backseat of the family van motoring down the interstate.

Back at home, if the television isn't on, then maybe the personal computer is. Have you ever walked into a room while someone is tapping on the keyboard, eyes riveted to the screen?

If I may, let me suggest something radical: Turn it off. Have a talk.

My brother, Dan, is in the bridge-building business. The engineering company he works for is responsible for designing some of the most spectacular spans in the world. But as amazing as these structures are, there's nothing more magnificent than the bridge called conversation—the magic link that connects one person to another.

On this bridge, words travel back and forth—thoughts, ideas, concerns, affirmations and thanks. When these words are able to journey from one person to another without any noisy distractions, their safe arrival is almost always ensured.

You may never have thought of it this way, but you and my brother have something in common. As a dad, you're in the bridge-building business, too. And mealtime is a terrific place to start construction.

> *Blessed are all who fear the LORD, who walk in his ways.*
>
> *Your sons will be like olive shoots around your table.*
>
> *Thus is the man blessed who fears the LORD.*

PSALM 128:1, 3–4

In addition to the dinner table, driving along in the car is another good place to do some bridge building. Or how about an evening with a checker board spread out on the floor between you rather than staring at the television?

Sometimes the best way to get these bridges started is with good questions: "What was the best thing that happened to you today?" Or you can set yourself up with a good one like, "Do you know why I'm so proud of you?" Then when your child says, "No," you can let 'em have it with lots of great stuff!

One of the things I like about the story of the two friends walking to Emmaus is that they weren't sitting across a table, staring at each other. Sometimes conversation works best when there's something else—non electronic—going on: walking, fishing, building something together, watching ducks from a park bench, painting a fence, or playing in the sand at the beach.

When your children have grown, the bridge-building investment you make in them now will ensure your words a smooth ride. Getting together or picking up the phone when they call will connect two friends whose relationship is strong and sure.

In the past God spoke to our forefathers

through the prophets at many times and in various ways,

but in these last days

He has spoken to us by his Son.

HEBREWS 1:1–2

The Prayers

A PRAYER *for* YOU

Father in Heaven,

You are a God of relationships. You listen for my voice and speak to me. You answer and you ask. Thank you for building the relationship bridge with me through the conversation of prayer. Thank you for your Spirit that explains your Word for my understanding. I commit to turn off the gadgets in my life long enough to have focused conversation with you. I commit to building bridges with my children so words can travel back and forth between us. I promise to begin to find times away from distractions to link our hearts in the ordinary moments of our lives with conversation. I need your help to be aware of the time, places and questions that lead to real communication. With your help, I can build a bridge that will span a lifetime with my child.

In the strong name of Jesus,

Amen.

A Prayer *for* Your Child

Father in Heaven,

You are a God of relationships. You want a connection with my child that is full of two-way conversations. Thank you for providing words—written and spoken—to build a link to her heart. Thank you for your Spirit that speaks to my child's heart and helps her to understand your Word. Thank you for my child's prayers that link her to you every mealtime and every time she desires to talk to you. Help my child value quiet moments without electronic distractions. As she learns from me what it's like to discuss things, let her build bridges of conversation in her relationship with you. Thank you for your voice that is with her when I cannot be.

In the strong name of Jesus,

Amen.

Ideal conversation must be an exchange of thought, and not, as many of those who worry most about their shortcomings believe, an eloquent exhibition of wit or oratory.

Emily Post

WHAT'S *that* SMELL?

The Promise

Thanks be to God,
Who always leads us in triumphal procession in Christ
and through us spreads everywhere the fragrance of the knowledge of him.
For we are to God the aroma of Christ
among those who are being saved and those who are perishing.

2 CORINTHIANS 2:14–15

The Picture

Biology was my favorite subject in high school. The study of God's plant and animal creation completely captured me.

When we got to the human body, one of the things I remember studying was the power of the olfactory system. Of the five senses—smelling, touching, seeing, hearing, and tasting—the system of smell is the one with the best memory.

What this means is that when you smell mothballs or a cedar closet, it may bring back decades-old childhood memories of visits to grandma's house. A certain cologne or perfume will remind you years later of the person who wore it. Smells from the kitchen can take you back to your parents' home. No other sense alerts this depth of recall.

The hillsides in the Provence region of France are carpeted with the elegant spikes of the lavender flower. Small factories dot the landscape, turning the purple flower into one of the most fragrant oils in the world.

At the end of the workday, employees from these factories make their way home through the streets of the villages. The townspeople don't need to be told that the lavender factories have closed for the day. Because of the pungent aroma that rises from the workers heading home, they can literally *smell* what time it is.

Do you know that your home smells like something?

When you and your children leave your home to travel to school or work, what's your fragrance? Does your home have the aroma of Christ—grace, tenderness, thoughtfulness, encouraging words, kind deeds, and laughter?

If you could use some air fresheners with your family, here are some ideas that will keep your home smelling wonderful. These are words you can speak to your family that will saturate the atmosphere:

"I love you."

No three words create more magic than these.

"I need your love."

Unmet expectations can crush a spirit. Tell your family what you need. ("I need a hug," was a common one in our home.)

"I'm sorry; I was wrong; will you please forgive me."

These words may be the most difficult you've ever spoken. But healing begins once you've said them all.

"May I help?"

Laziness is a family's great enemy. There's lots of work to do around your place. Pitch in.

"Thank you."

No words are more encouraging than these. Look for opportunities to say them.

Words like these—and some others I'm sure you can think of—will fill your home with an incredible fragrance.

Oh, there is one more thing. One of the interesting qualities of the sense of smell is that it also the one that fatigues most quickly. In other words, when you walk into a room where someone has one of those electronic room deodorizers, you can smell it right away. But in no time at all, the smell is gone. Your nose gets accustomed to the scent, and you can't detect it any more.

When you take your wife on a date and she sprays on her favorite perfume, you only smell it for a short time. This smelling sense gets tired. So you can't depend on yesterday's aroma in your home to last until tomorrow. You've got to renew it every day. Now you know how.

Live a life of love,
just as Christ loved us and gave himself up for us
as a fragrant offering and sacrifice to God.

Ephesians 5:2

The Prayers

A PRAYER *for* YOU

Father in Heaven,

I want our home to have the sweet aroma that comes from living in your kingdom. I want the memories to smell good for a long time so my children remember love and kindness, laughter and encouragement. I need to take out the garbage of bitterness and selfishness. Let me be the first one to fill our home with gracious words, hugs, smiles, and service. May everyone who enters our home smell the goodness of your Spirit. And as we leave our home, let the fragrance be so enticing, that others are drawn to you because we smell so good.

For your glory.

Amen

A PRAYER *for* YOUR CHILD

Father in Heaven,

My child needs to smell good and I'm the one who will be pouring the fragrance of your love on him. Help my child to put on love so he smells wonderful. Help him put on smiles so that he is a winsome witness of the joy you give. With a grateful heart, help him to be a servant who will delight everyone's senses. Thank you for the fun of living and working in the scent of your Spirit.

You're an amazing God.

Amen

Nothing smells so fragrant
as the forgiven soul
standing before the throne of God.

EMMA DURKINS

WITH a TOUCH

The Promise

The one who looked like a man touched me and gave me strength.

"Do not be afraid, O man highly esteemed," he said.

"Peace! Be strong now; be strong."

When he spoke to me, I was strengthened and said,

"Speak, my lord, since you have given me strength."

DANIEL 10:18–19

The Picture

Without a touch, children die.

The story is told of Fredrick II, king of France in the early thirteenth century.[1] A vigorous nationalist, he was determined to establish French as the preferred language of all mankind. His theory was that when children were born, French was their default language. Any other tongue had to be taught, but French came naturally.

He commissioned an experiment. Three newborn babies were placed in cribs. They had no regular contact with humans—no speaking or touching. Frederick postulated that the children would begin speaking French, rather than Latin, Hebrew, or God forbid, English.

However, Frederick's test failed. Before they were old enough to speak, without the touch of a human being, each of the children perished.

One of the things that fascinates me about Jesus' life and work was his interest in touching. As God, he could have healed the sick with laser beams or commanded his understudies to embrace the children. But he didn't. He healed the sick and raised the dead with a touch.

I used to think that touching was primarily a woman-thing. Only men who were in regular contact with their feminine side were comfortable with the whole idea. This is a false notion.

The next time you're watching a major league baseball game and one of the players slams a line drive into the center field bleachers, watch what happens as he circles the bases. The first base coach shakes his hand and slaps him on the rump as he rounds first. The third base coach does the same as he heads for home. His teammate on deck gives him a high five and then when he reaches the dugout, every one of his teammates—every single one of them—pat him on the back, sock him on the arm, or tousle his hair.

The very same thing is true when a basketball coach calls a time out and the players head for the bench. If they've just captured the lead, their teammates will explode from their seats and slap the players in celebration. Football players who catch the touchdown pass or make the spectacular game-saving tackle face the same fate when they return to their benches.

Even golf pros and their caddies exchange handshakes and hugs when the ball drops in the cup after a great shot.

All of these celebrations are about touching. And these touches send a powerful message to each man. It rewards the one receiving the touches—"I did a good job." And it rewards those who are doing the touching—"I'm so proud to be on your team." These simple acts of touching are, pure and simple, the transmission of a blessing.

Why is touching so important? You may know that there are more nerve endings clustered at the end of your fingers than anywhere in your body. You can run your finger over a piece of smooth glass and detect a scratch no more than 1/2500th of an inch deep. Nothing on your body is more sensitive than your fingertips, but the gift of touching is more than just a certain sensitivity.

The tender touch of a father's hand on his child's face transmits a special kind of love. Taking the hand of a six-year-old daughter gives her confidence. The tussle of a dad with his son on the family room floor communicates manly strength and security. The hugs of a father can comfort a teenager's broken heart. The intimate touch of a man to his wife connects their souls.

Many times throughout the Bible, a touch meant the transmission of a blessing. From father to son, the blessing was passed along with a touch. Abraham blessed Isaac, Isaac blessed Jacob, and Jacob blessed each of his twelve sons. This happened over and over again throughout recorded Scripture. In fact, in one biblical account, parents brought little children to Jesus for that very purpose. Jesus conveyed a sacramental blessing on these children, and he did it with a touch.

As our children's father, we have the right and the privilege of blessing our children. And we can do it as Jesus did it . . . with a tender, godly, life-giving touch.

Jesus reached out his hand and touched the man.

The Prayers

A PRAYER *for* YOU

Heavenly Father,

Thank you for the example of Jesus who blessed people wherever he went with a touch. Your tenderness transmitted your love and care. You continue to touch me with the warmth of your Holy Spirit. Thank you for the confidence your touch creates. I want to be like you and hold my children. I want them to feel my blessing and yours. Today, help me to be aware of who needs a hug, or a pat, or a demonstration of love in a touch. Thank you for the privilege of blessing each of my children with the connection of a loving touch.

In the comfort of your blessing,

Amen.

A Prayer *for* Your Child

Father in Heaven,

Thank you for making my child sensitive to tenderness and touch. Today, help my child to feel the security of my love through my affection and hugs. Bless my child with confidence in your unconditional love and mine, too. Wrap her up in the warmth of your Spirit and my gentleness. May the words of blessing my child hears from me be written on her soul because I seal it with a tender touch.

With confidence in your promise,

Amen.

Affection is responsible for nine-tenths of whatever solid and durable happiness there is in our lives.

C.S. Lewis

LOOKING UP

The Promise

Those who look to him are radiant;
their faces are never covered with shame.

PSALM 34:5

The Picture

"All right men, we're going to count off by two's . . . ready? Go."

"1" "2" "1" "2" "1" "2" "1"

All dads can be divided into two groups. The guys in Group One have been good dads. Group Two needs improvement. Group One has given their children an endowment that will make a vast contribution to their futures. Group Two has not.

The dads in Group One realized, early in their child's development, that this gift would not come naturally. It had to be delivered in specific detail. And so they did it. The fathers in Group Two hoped that their children would pick it up naturally. Of course, very few did.

You can spot the children of the guys in Group One. You may bump into them at the park or grocery store or hanging around your neighborhood on their bicycles. And you can tell that their dads are in Group One by simply speaking to them.

"Hello, Kyle," you say.

"Hi, Mr. Jones," they respond. "How are you?" These children look at you while they're speaking.

"Fine," you answer. "It's a great day, isn't it?"

"Yes sir." And Kyle rides on.

But when you talk to the children of the dads in Group Two, they suddenly become fascinated with the floor.

"Hello, Eddie," you say.

"Hrumph eck morshuptel schurpt," he mumbles to his shoe tops.

"I hope you're doing okay," you say, trying to crowbar something understandable out of him—something in a language you're familiar with.

"Brelobth drunchet trop," he responds.

No luck.

Eddie shuffles off.

Who taught this child to speak like that? you wonder to yourself. And then, since you're one smart man you settle on the answer. *No* one taught him … and *that's* the problem with the guys in Group Two.

When it comes to learning to communicate (I didn't say "talk") most children are born with a blank slate. Of course, there are exceptions. Some kids emerge from the womb ready to host their own quiz show. But most are in need of help. And it's *your* job to teach them.

As soon as they begin to talk, you start playing conversational games. You can pick out one of their favorite stuffed animals or space men and you pretend that you're meeting them for the first time. You go first.

"Hello, BooBoo Bear," you say, taking the animal's paw in your hand and shaking it. You make sure that your child sees that you're looking right into the bear's button eyes when you're talking to him.

"Hello, Mr. Jones," you answer, using your Mickey Mouse voice.

Once you've finished with a simple dialogue, you give your tike a shot at it so he can practice what you've just demonstrated. Then you look for a chance for your child to use what he's learning, in live action. You introduce him to one of your friends at church.

You pay close attention to how well your child is learning this skill and you help him once your friend has moved on. "That was good," you say, "But the next time be sure to look right into the man's eyes when you talk to him ... just like I did with BooBoo Bear."

Congratulations and welcome to Group One.

Zachary Britt is one of my favorite neighbor kids. He and his parents, Stan and Debbie, live right across the street from us. At age seven, Zach is one incredibly active boy. Whether he's scooting around on his roller blades, skateboard or his bicycle, he's Mr. Perpetual Motion.

I often see Zachary when I'm walking our dog or headed to the mailbox. "Hello, Zachary," I say.

Zach looks up and gives me a big smile. "Hello, Mr. Robert," he says.

Zachary's dad is obviously in Group One!

When you stop and think about it, teaching your children the proper way to speak to a grown up is another terrific way to show them how to pray.

Father, may your name be honored.

May your Kingdom come.

LUKE 11:2, GNT

Notes

A Conundrum *for* Sure

i Please don't give me too much credit here. We had driven back and forth on this highway on our summer and holiday visits to Bobbie's family for over twenty years—hence, the "Could we stop *this time*."

And *in* Your Purity

ii Admittedly, some boys told our daughters that if they had to be interviewed by their dad, they were not interested in taking them out. This was not a problem for them . . . or for me.

Are You Fun *to* Live With?

iii A hen has no teeth.

2 How about the time when two roaches were munching on garbage in the alley. "I was in that new restaurant across the street," one of them said to the other. "It's so clean! The kitchen is spotless, the floors are gleaming white. It's so sanitary the whole place shines." "Please," said the other roach. "Not while I'm eating."

Expect *and* Inspect

iv See Exodus 35 through 39.

2 Exodus 39:43

Family Secrets

v If you're interested, I'll be happy to tell you about the other "family secrets" on our list like, "There's a person named Eunice?" "Is that yo Muh-thuh?" "It's a pink suitcase;" or "Schnoopsh." If you're *not* interested, I understand.

For Just One Weekend

vi I did break 80 one time and it only took me 15 holes to do it.

2 These superlatives were provided to me by my friend and PGA pro, Brad Brewer, one of golf's finest instructors!

I *a* Cwistian

vii I'm talking about first things/new things here. Our second daughter, Julie, was born on October 25, 1974 and this, of course, was thrilling, too.

2 John 3:5-7

3 Matthew 19:13-15, Mark 10:13-16, Luke 18:15-17

4 Mark 9:22b

5 According to the original texts, these figures were not present at the manger scene in Bethlehem.

6 Some doctrinal judgments were being made here.

Just Walk Behind *the* Plow

1 His daddy was the pastor of the *Mount Pleasan*t Brethren in Christ Church in *Mount Joy*. "Where never was heard a discouraging word and the skies were not cloudy all day."

2 Mark 4

Prophet, Priest *and* King

1 Exodus 28:21

Put *it in* Writing

1 Note: If you have a son and he's sixteen or older, the lunch-napkin-note may not be a good idea.

2 R.C. Sproul and Robert Wolgemuth, *What's in the Bible* (Nashville, TN: Word Publishing, 2001) page 229.

The Birds *and* Bees

1 Enrique Bermudez–Correspondent in Argentina Pedro Iribarren, Director/Proprietor of the journal NUEVA ETAPA of Mar de Plata, Argentina translation by Charles Heizman.

The Door

1 Exodus 12:7

2 Deuteronomy 6:9

3 Luke 13:24-27

4 Revelation 3:20

Turn It Off, Have *a* Talk

1 Luke 24:31

With *a* Touch

1 I read about Frederick II's shenanigans in a *Psychology Today* article 25 years ago. He was also known as Frederick the Stupid.

Also Available from Inspirio:

DAD'S PRAYERS FROM THE HEART
A Guided Journal

PRAYERS FROM A MOM'S HEART
Asking God's Blessing and Protection for Your Children
by Fern Nichols

MOM'S PRAYERS FROM THE HEART
A Guided Journal

PRAYERS FROM A GRANDMA'S HEART
Asking God's Blessing and Protection
for all Your Grandchildren
by Quin Sherrer

GRANDMA'S PRAYERS FROM THE HEART
A Guided Journal